The making of Egypt

Egypt belongs to the earliest and highest civilised cultures of the ancient World. Five thousand years ago Egypt was the dominant World power, while in America, Europe and Asia roamed hunters who belonged to pre-historic era. At the same time ancient Egyptians had discovered agriculture and invented the script. Through astronomical observation they determined the solar year as 365 days, which they further divided into months and weeks. A day was defined as twelve day light hours and twelve night hours. The hour was their smallest time unit. They knew also how to melt copper, and to mine gold and make jewelry, and also to glaze stone surfaces. In agriculture they invented the pickaxe and made experiments on plants and animals.

Geographically Egypt is isolated from the rest of the World. From the south and west the barren desert has kept it away from any intruders. From the north and east the sea has contributed to its isolation. The peninsula of Sinai presented the only gateway to the civilised World at the time. Thousands of years later invaders reached Egypt through Sinai, and it was also through Sinai that the Egyptian army ruled the East. So Egypt had well defined physical boundaries. Within this well defined boundary the country was further divided to Upper and Lower Egypt. Upper Egypt was a narrow strip of land on the banks of the Nile stretching from the First Cataract till Memphis, a distance of about 900 km. Lower Egypt is a fertile river delta in the form of a triangle stretching for 200 km. Its northern boundary is where the Nile flows into the Mediterranean. The monsoon rain at the Ethiopian mountains from July till September resulted in heavy floods in Egypt where the Nile carried the fertile soil from the Ethiopian mountains into the desert land of Egypt thus creating the biggest and most fertile oasis of the World.

The first inhabitants of north Africa were hunters, and the population of Egypt was a mixture of Africans and Asiatics who moved to Egypt through Sinai. Ten to fifteen thousand years ago rain ceased from the regions today known as the Eastern and Western Desert. As a response the population slowly moved towards the Nile Valley and started agriculture and animal farming. They gave up the nomadic style of life and started to live in communities. At this moment civilisation was born. Until then the Nile Valley was regarded as dangerous swamps full of beasts such as crocodiles, hippos, and big cats. The Nile flooded in July and all low lands were covered in water, therefore the inhabitants were obliged to move to higher places and perhaps resumed again their habit of hunting till the flood dropped.

The lives of the ancient Egyptians was thus based on a constant rhythm that was basically influenced on by two factors namely sun and flood. Both powers had an inherit destructive agent. For example a strong sun will burn the agricultural products, and the lack of sun in winter could result in freezing of plantation and hence equally in ruining them. Similarly a strong flood would drown villages and corps, and a week flood will result in hunger. Both of these phenomena contributed in strengthening the idea of death and rebirth. Each evening the ancient Egyptians observed the sun setting beyond the western horizon, hence linked to the symbol of death, and at dawn they observed the sun rise from the eastern horizon, which was associated with the symbol of reb[...] flood cycle they believed tha[...]

Later in the historic perio[...] nomic system and learned ho[...] nomic scale thus preventing [...] crucial factor in the development of civilisation. Through the economic system people had more time and means that resulted in the birth of different specialised professions in arts, mining, engineering and management. Isolated settlements were united in villages which in turn were developed into towns and trade centres. Common interest of individuals resulted in forming social habits. The rich and powerful settlements assumed the lead over isolated settlements. The most famous settlement in Upper Egypt was Nekhen which had the White Crown as emblem. The capital of Lower Egypt was Buto who had the Red Crown as emblem, and its symbol was the bee. At that point of history all the settlements and little kingdoms were united into two Kingdoms Upper and Lower Egypt. The history of ancient Egypt starts at the point where the two kingdoms were united by Narmer in c. 3200 BC. and ends when Alexander the Great conquered Egypt in 332 BC.

Geography

The area of Egypt measures one million square Km and lies in the driest part of Africa. To north it is bounded by the Mediterranean sea and to the east by the Red Sea. Both seas are separated by the peninsula of Sinai. When the Nile enters Egypt it has already flown for 5000 km from its source. Through millions of years the Nile has forced its way through the rocks. The rock-cut temple of Abu Simbel with its four guardian statues was built by Ramses II more than 3000 years ago stands welcoming the Nile and guarding Egypt's southern borders. It was carved from a rock overlooking the Nile. Forty years ago it has been removed into an artificial rock overlooking an artificial lake. But the temple has lost nothing of its majestical powers. The artificial lake is 'Lake Nasser', it stores the flood water.

The Nile and its valley is not only what makes up Egypt. Deep in the desert are beautiful oasis of luxuriant green. Another wonderful fauna lies in the coral reefs of the Red Sea. The coral reef teems with life in marked contrast to the barren desert shores.

The Great Pyramid of Khufo

The Great Pyramid is the oldest of the Seven Wonders of the ancient world. It still stands defying time. In fact, it was built to outlive all of humanity. The Great Pyramid is a perfect building and yet so enormous that its construction would exhaust the skills and resources of today's technology almost to breaking point. Yet it is astonishing, and one can find no explanation for the fact that only a hundred years separate this giant building from the construction of Pharaoh Djoser's Step Pyramid at Sakkara, the first large stone building ever raised on earth. And only a couple of centuries separate the Great Pyramid's age from the edge of pre-history.

The present height is 137.38m, made up of 203 courses of masonry. The summit has a base length of 14.55m. The height of the pyramid as originally built was 146.649m, and the side length is 235.5 m. The faces have an inclination of 51° 51′ to the horizontal. It has been verified that the ratio of the Great Pyramid's perimeter to its height equals 2pi, which is the ratio of a circle's circumference to its diameter.

The precision with which the Great Pyramid was built is still, with today's technology, a source of great fascination. It is likely that the experimental phase of Cheops's father Pharaoh Snefru was the main driving force for this precision in work. This precision produced a pyramid whose base level difference in height is less than 2.1cm, and the maximum difference in length between the sides is 4.4cm. The blocks used in the pyramid have an average weight of 2.5 tons, decreasing in size towards the top. Some of the casing stones at the base are very large, weighing as much as 15 tons. The heaviest blocks are of granite, used as the roof of the King's Chamber and as weight-carrying support. Their weigh is estimated as 50 - 80 tons each.

Herodotus and the Arab travellers refer to the inscriptions covering the casing stone outside of the Great Pyramid that if copied would fill over 10000 pages. The casing stone was removed in the 13th century to build Cairo houses. Since then the Great Pyramid has the shape that we see today.

In my opinion Cheops, who was able to undertake such vast work, was the most powerful human being that the world has ever seen. Nothing much is known about Khufo, he was the son of King Snefru and Queen Hetepheres daughter and heiress of Huni. Herodotus wrote that Khufo was a tyrant, because he enslaved the whole country to built his pyramid project.

Left : the Giza Pyramids.
Civilisation that had long disappeared, the three Giza Pyramids stand in breathtaking geometrical symmetry. In the foreground before Mycerinus's Pyramid, the smallest of the three, are the satellite tombs of his family. Chephren's pyramid (centre), with its original limestone cap still in place, appears larger than the Great Pyramid to the rear because it is built on a higher ground.
About 4,700 years ago, Egypt entered an era of great technological progress. Until about 3000 BC, the basic building material was sun-dried brick. About 200 years later the Pyramids of Giza were built of stone blocks, weighing on the average 15 tons each and fitted together with great precision. The techniques of constructing these great monuments were invented by Imhotep, the vizier of Pharaoh Djoser. At Sakkara, using small stone blocks instead of traditional mud bricks, Imhotep built the Step Pyramid and the funerary temple. Nothing similar to these buildings had ever been built on earth.

This argument is now rejected owing to the great precision and technology involved, reflecting that it has been built only out of love or worshipping a divine ruler.

The building of the Great Pyramid was a miracle of organisation; the final facing of the sides of the pyramid with smooth and perfectly joined blocks is evidence of the finest craftsmanship. The internal passages and burial chamber were built with unmatched skill, the joints between the huge blocks being almost invisible. The entrance was placed high up in the north side; and after the burial it was closed with masonry similar to that of the whole casing of the surface, so that there was no indication of its position in the glass-smooth and inaccessible face of the pyramid.

The workmen used tools made of bronze. The jewelled cutting joints may have been of beryl, topaz or sapphire. For cutting the stones they employed great bronze saws with jewelled cutting points. In some places, e.g. the granite sarcophagus of Cheops, the marks made by these saws can be clearly seen. By curving the saw-blades into a circle drills were formed, which could cut out a circular hole by rotation. For smaller objects the cutting edge was held stationary while the work was revolved; 'the lathe' says Petrie, "appears to have been as familiar an instrument in the 4th Dynasty as in our modern workshops". Some of the superb diorite bowls must have been turned. They are too accurate to have been made by hand. Though the chisels have been found, no examples of jewelled saws and drills have been discovered, but this is not surprising as owing to their value they would be carefully looked after, and when worn the jewels removed and placed in new tools.

3

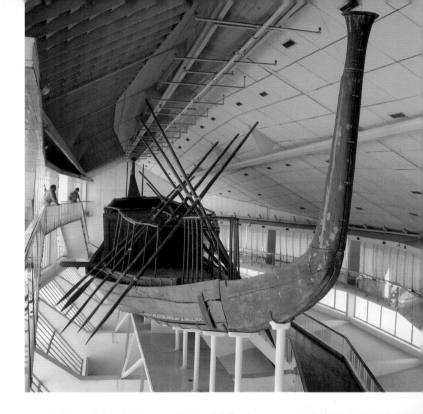

Left : the Great Pyramid of Khufo.

Top right : in the Old Kingdom it was customary to bury funerary boats near the burial monument. A number of empty boat-shaped pits occur around the Great Pyramid. In 1954 two intact boats on the south side of the pyramid were discovered. The pit was closed by 41 limestone blocks, each weighing 16 tons, and completely sealed with plaster. A smaller keying block at one end had to be removed, before any of the larger ones could be lifted. The pit is rectangular and not boat-shaped.

When opened, two dismantled cedarwood boats were discovered, the oldest boats of that size to be found so far. The pit was 30m long, and the boat after it had been assembled was 43.2m long. A large cabin was placed a little after midship on the deck, its roof supported by palm-shaped columns. The timber was held together by wood pins and ropes. Ahmed Youssef was responsible for the ingenious work of restoring and reassembling the vessel. He was also responsible for much of the work on the furniture of Queen Hetepheres.

The burial of the boats was performed by Cheops's successor Djedefre. An inscription on the blocks reads 'Re-djed--ef is the ruler'. This must have been carried out by some of the workmen.

Right : despite Cheops's achievement of building his Great Pyramid, the only surviving statue of him is an ivory one 7.5cm long and found by Petrie at Abydos in 1903. During excavation at the Temple of Osiris at Kom al-Sultan close to Abydos one of his workmen brought him a headless statue of a man seated on a throne. From the hieroglyphic inscription Petrie immediately recognised that it was Cheops. He ordered all his men immediately to sift through the rubble that had been cast away in search of the head, offering a reward to the finder. Finally, after three weeks of intensive work, the head was found. The face in the statue is strong, and conveys vividly an impression of a monarch who exercised absolute power.

Pyramid of Chephren, Great is Khafre

The second largest pyramid of the group was built in 2550 BC by the Pharaoh Chephren (Khafre in ancient Egyptian). It lies to the south-west of Cheops's pyramid, on the prolongation of the diagonal of that structure. To the ancient Egyptians it was known as Wer-Khafre, meaning 'Khafre is Great'.

In size it is not quite so overpowering as that of Cheops, but since it is built on higher ground it appears even larger, especially when viewed from the southern, desert side. Each side measured 215 metres, but is now 211 metres long, and inclined at an angle of 53° 7′.

To the south is a small pyramid, the tomb of the queen, and to the east lies the mortuary temple, now in almost complete ruin. From there, a causeway leads to the temple of the Sphinx or granite Temple. The pyramid's height is 144 metres, and it retains virtually its full height by the preservation of the limestone casing at the building's apex. The lowest course of the pyramid's 'outer skin' is composed of red granite blocks, best preserved at the western end of the south side.

Chephren, the son of Cheops, came to the throne after the death of his elder brother Pharaoh Djedefre, who ruled only briefly. He returned the royal necropolis to Giza and built a pyramid there next to his father's. He built the valley temple with granite, and also carved the biggest and most famous sculpture of all times—the Great Sphinx. This is 72m long, and has Chephren's head and the body of a recumbent lion.

Left : the Pyramid of Chephren.
Right : the magnificent diorite statue of Pharaoh Chephren. This hard stone has been worked with excellent skill. The smoothly polished surface gives a natural appeal to the muscular body. The viewer is left in awe as he stands in front of this spectacular statue, which gives the feeling of looking at a divine ruler. The features of Chephren in the statue are very similar to those of his Sphinx. In both he wears the *nemes* headdress ornamented with a cobra. The Pharaoh, his face dressed up with a false beared, sits on his throne with a slightly dreamy look in his eyes. In his right hand he once had a flail, the symbol of the wealth coming from the soil of the Nile Valley.
This statue was found at the valley temple of his pyramid, one of 23 statues that once stood there. All were ruined in ancient times; Egyptian Museum in Cairo.

The Egyptian Museum in Cairo

1. Narmer's Palette

c. 3200 BC. Ground floor, gallery 43;

Smiting the enemy, Pharaoh Narmer is represented as the Pharaoh of both Upper and Lower Egypt and battles to unite the Two Lands under his rule. This First Dynasty commemorative palette is one of Egypt's oldest surviving historical records. It was found in Hierakonpolis, the ancient capital of Upper Egypt.

Here the Pharaoh, wearing the White Crown of Upper Egypt, is about to smash with a club the head of his enemy, probably an inhabitant of Lower Egypt. This representation became a standard symbol in Egyptian art for the next 3,000 years. The Pharaoh here is also decorated with an animal tail and is followed by his sandal-bearer. Above the enemy is the Pharaoh incarnated as the hawk-god, Horus, holding the enemy with a rope with his strong right hand. The enemy is within the papyrus marches of the Delta. The hawk symbolises 'the god Horus', i.e. the divine representation of the Pharaoh, and the papyrus means Lower Egypt. One can therefore explain this emblem as Pharaoh Narmer conquering the Delta. Two bearded men, enemies of the Pharaoh, are fleeing naked, possibly running or swimming, or are, as most see it, lying dead on the ground.

2. Pharaoh Khasekhem, Horus-Seth Khasekhem (the powerful one appears)

c. 2714 - 2687 BC. Ground floor, gallery 48;

This statue of is one of the first statues of a Pharaoh. It was found in Hierakonpolis. Here the Pharaoh wears the White Crown of Upper Egypt. The head is tilted forward to balance the mass of the White Crown. His left arm is folded across his waist while his right arm stretches on his thigh. The right part of the face including the nose were ruined in antiquity. The small remaining part of the face, specially the details of the eye and the muscles show the magnificent work of sculpture. It is carved with great care and is extremely expressive.

On the lower sides of the statue are drawings showing the Pharaoh smiting his enemy which are probably citizens of Lower Egypt. The inscription states that the pharaoh had captured 47209 of his enemies.

3. Pharaoh Djoser, Horus Netjery-Khet

3rd Dynasty, 2668 - 2649 BC. Ground floor, gallery 43;

The limestone statue of Pharaoh Djoser was found in a *serdab* next to his Step Pyramid of Sakkara. He is represented seated, wearing the garment of the jubilee festival. His royal head cover extends to his neck but does not conceal his ears. Originally the statue was covered with plaster and was painted. The inscription on the base reads the royal Horus name Netjery-khet. The crystal eyes were taken away by robbers. The Turin Papyrus states that Djoser reigned for 19 years and was titled 'Pharaoh of Upper and Lower Egypt'.

4. King Chephren

4th Dynasty, reign of Chephren 2576 - 2551 BC. Ground floor, room 42

5 & 6. Limestone pair statues of Prince Ra-Hotep and his wife Nofert.

Reign of Snefru, 2649 - 2609 BC., Ground floor, gallery 32;

The two figures are represented seated on a square cut chair. The statues are painted, the eyes are inlaid with crystal and outlined with black. Nofert wears a necklace, and surmounting her head is a heavy black wig that reaches her shoulders. On her forehead is a band ornamented with a floral design. The pair statues found near the Pyramid of Meidum, is regarded as one of the magnificent statues of the Old Kingdom, *c.* 2600 BC.

7. Seated Scribe

5th Dynasty, *c.* 2460 BC. Ground floor room 42, Painted limestone.

The seated scribe has a scroll of papyrus on his lap, and is ready to write with his right hand. But the pen has disappeared. His hair is black, head and neck are orange-brown coloured, the rest of the body lighter coloured with less orange tan. An unfinished band around the neck represents a necklace. He has inlaid eyes, fringed with copper representing eye-paint. The lower part of the body and legs are a little rough.

8. Ka-aper, called Sheikh el-Balad

5th Dynasty, reign of Userkaf 2513 - 2506 BC. Ground floor, room 42;

This wooden statue of a priest shows him in a realistic style with a large stomach. His eyes are inlaid with white quartz, crystal and resin and surrounded by a copper frame. This statue is one of the most magnificent non-royal statues of the Old Kingdom. Standing in front of this statue the viewer is left in awe. It realises the ancient Egyptian definition of eternity. It seems so real that one thinks that the priest is standing live in front of us, and that he will live forever.

9. Head of a falcon

6th Dynasty *c.* 2350 BC. Upper floor, room 4.

This magnificent piece was discovered by Quibell in 1897. It was part of a bronze statue of the falcon god Horus of Nekhen. The head is chiselled from a single piece of gold. The beak is a second piece of gold that had been soldered into the head. The eyes are not made of two pieces of stones as one would imagine but of a single rod of obsidian. The curvature of both ends is polished in such a way to resemble the ferocious stare of a bird of prey. The crown and *uraeus* are fixed with rivets to the head. It is possible that the crown and *uraeus* were part of an interchangeable ornament that were surmounting the cult statue according to different events. Other crowns could include the solar disk, the White Crown, the Blue Crown, or the *atef* Crown. The body of the falcon is made of copper, and the head was fixed to the body with copper rivets.

10. The Triad of Mycerinus

4th Dynasty, reign of Mycerinus 2551 - 2523 BC. Ground floor, gallery 47.

This is a group of three statues. In the centre is the Pharaoh Mycerinus wearing the White Crown of Upper Egypt. On his right stands goddess Hathor, goddess of the sky and of love. On her head she wears her characteristic emblem, the solar disk between two cow's horns. On Mycerinus's left side stands a different figure in each of the three statues.

11. Granite head of Userkaf

5th Dynasty, reign of Userkaf 2498 - 2513 BC. Ground floor, gallery 46.

12. Head of Pharaoh Userkaf

5th Dynasty, reign of Userkaf 2498 - 2513 BC. Ground floor, gallery 47.

Pharaoh Userkaf, founder of the Fifth Dynasty, sculpted in schist. The eyebrows are elongated. The statue was found at the sun temple at Abusir in 1957. It is very rare for Old Kingdom sculpture to represent a Pharaoh wearing the crown of Lower Egypt.

13. Limestone statue of a seated scribe

5th Dynasty, *c.* 2450 BC. Ground floor, room 42.

The head is in proportion large compared with the body. The face is excellently sculpted. The eyes are inlaid, with a copper line. The ornaments of the ear are also of copper. The statue was found in Sakkara close to the seated scribe.

14. The Scribe

5th Dynasty, *c.* 2450 BC. Ground floor, gallery 46.

15. Reserve head,

4th Dynasty, *c.* 2600 BC. Ground floor gallery 46.

16. Amenemhat III,

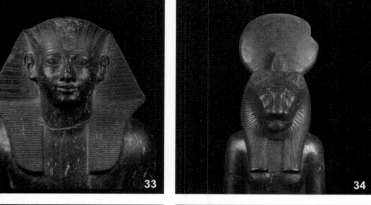

12th Dynasty, reign of Amenemhat III 1843 - 1797 BC. Ground floor Gallery 16.

17. Statue of Mentuhotep Nebhepetre
11th Dynasty reign of Mentuhotep II 2061 - 2010 BC. Ground floor, gallery 26.

18. Wooden statue of Senusert I
12th Dynasty, reign of Senusert I, 1971 - 1928 BC. Ground floor, room 22.

19. Senusert III
12th Dynasty, reign of Senusert III, 1878 - 1843 BC. Ground floor, gallery 21.

20. Amenemhat III in priestly costume
12th Dynasty, reign of Amenemhat III, 1843 - 1797 BC. Ground floor, gallery 21.

21. Double statue of Amenemhat III as a Nile god
12th Dynasty, reign of Amenemhat III, 1843 - 1797 BC. Ground floor, gallery 21.

22. Queen Nefert
12th Dynasty, reign of Senusert II, 1897 - 1877 BC. Ground floor, gallery 26.

23. *Ka* statue of Hor Auibre
13th Dynasty, reign of Auibre, *c.* 1700 BC. Ground floor, gallery 16.

24. Troop of Nubian archers
11th Dynasty, *c.* 2000 BC. Upper floor, room 37.

25. Offering bearer
11th Dynasty, *c.* 2000 BC. Upper floor, room 27.

26. Anthropoid coffin of Queen Ahhotep
18th Dynasty, reign of Ahmose, 1569 - 1545 BC. Upper floor, gallery 46.

27. Antropoid coffin of Queen Ahmose Merit Amun
18th Dynasty, reign of Amenhotep I, 1545 - 1525 BC. Upper floor gallery 46.

28. Head of Queen Hatshepsut
18th Dynasty, reign of Hatshepsut I, 1502 - 1482 BC. Ground floor gallery 11.

29. Head of Queen Hatshepsut from her granite Sphinx
18th Dynasty, reign of Hatshepsut I, 1502 - 1482 BC. Upper floor gallery 7.

30. Seated statue of Tuthmosis III
18th Dynasty, reign of Tuthmosis III, 1504 - 1452 BC. Ground floor room 12.

31. Bust of Tuthmosis III
18th Dynasty, reign of Tuthmosis III, 1504 - 1452 BC. Ground floor room 12.

32. Queen Isis, mother of Tuthmosis III
18th Dynasty, reign of Tuthmosis III, 1504 - 1452 BC. Ground floor room 12.

33. Amenhotep II with an offering Table
18th Dynasty, reign of Amenhotep II, 1454 - 1419 BC. Ground floor room 12.

34. Goddess Sekhmet
18th Dynasty, Ground floor gallery 6.

35. Coffin of Yuya
18th Dynasty, reign of Amenhotep III, 1410 - 1372 BC. Upper floor gallery 43.

36. Bust of Akhenaten
18th Dynasty, reign of Akhenaten, 1372 - 1355 BC. Ground floor room 3.

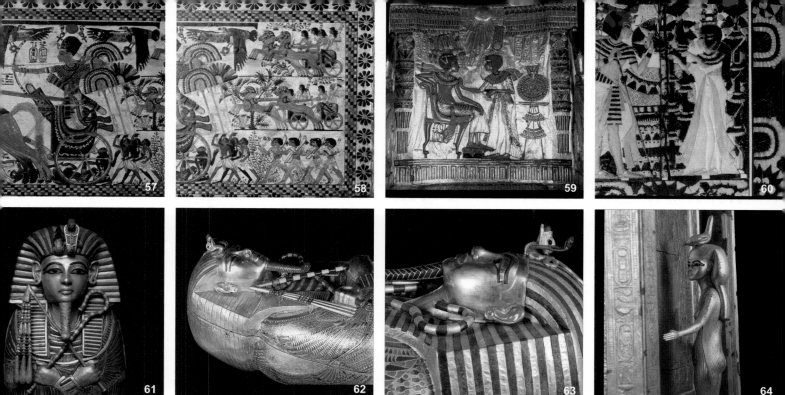

37. Akhenaten making an offering, Ground floor room 3.
38. Unfinished head of Nefertiti, Ground floor room 3.
39. Sculptor's model with two royal portraits, Ground floor room 3.
40. Detail from the Façade of a Shrine, Ground floor room 3.
41. Gold mask of Tutankhamun.
18th Dynasty, reign of Tutankhamun 1355 - 1346 BC. Upper floor room 3.
This magnificent funerary mask was fitted directly on the face and shoulders of the mummy lying in the innermost coffin. This mask is a perfect example of the goldsmith's extraordinary mastery of the art of the portrait. Life size, it is made of solid beaten gold and weighs 11 kilos and is inlaid with semi-precious stones and coloured glass. The eyes are inlaid with obsidian and quartz. In contrast to the coffins, it seems to have been made in the true image of the young sovereign. The golden mask thus showed the Pharaoh reborn and become divine flesh. The Pharaoh's face is framed by the *nemes* headdress, which he wears with the uraeus and vulture on the forehead symbolising the two protective deities of the unified Upper and Lower Egypt. The magic spell of Chapter 151 of the 'Book of the Dead' is inscribed on the back of the mask.
42 & 43. *Ka* statues of Tutankhamun, Upper floor gallery 45.
Two almost identical *ka* statues of Tutankhamun; in **43** he wears the *nemes* wig, in **42** he wears the *khat* wig. These statues were found at the entrance of the burial chamber as though guarding it. The statues are life-size and carved of wood. The statues are coloured black with bitumen. Black is the colour of the fertile land of Egypt, thus it became a symbol of resurrection and continuity of life. Osiris was sometimes represented in black, emphasising the belief that, after death, the king would personify Osiris, lord of the netherworld.

The *uraei* is placed on the forehead for protection. The eye lines and brows are inlaid with gilded bronze; and the eyes themselves with white quartz and obsidian.
44. Sekhmet, Upper floor gallery 45.
This statue of the goddess Sekhmet is made of gilded wood. Sekhmet has the body of a woman with a leonine head. Here Sekhmet is shown seated on her throne wearing the solar disk on her head. Sekhmet is a primary member of the Memphite Theology; she was the wife of Ptah and mother of Nefertum. She was the aggressive goddess of war who brought destruction to mankind. In New Kingdom funerary art she is shown standing on the solar boat to defend Ra from the Apophis snake. Ramses II wrote that Sekhmet joined him in his chariot and attacked the enemies with her fiery spitting. She represented the adverse aspects of the sun such as sunstroke, famine, drought and excessive heat.
45. Head of Tutankhamun emerging from the lotus flower, Upper floor gallery 20.
46 & 47. *Shawabti* of Tutankhamun, Upper floor gallery 40.
In **46** the king wears a nubian wig and in **47** he wears the Red Crown.
48. Detail of Tutankhamun's statue on a papyrus raft, Upper floor gallery 45.
49. Statue of Anubis, Upper floor gallery 9.
This is the most famous statue of Anubis. It is carved of wood and overlaid with black resin. It was found in the treasury room covered with a linen cloth, date marked to the seventh year of the reign of Akhenaten. A linen scarf like a leash was around his neck. Here he is represented wearing a collar crouching on his stomach upon a shrine-shaped chest. The outstanding details of the jackal's anatomy are an example of the great craftsmanship of the New Kingdom. His black colour was a symbol of fertility like the black fertile soil of Egypt. This statue has many characteristics of a dog; long muzzle, eyes with

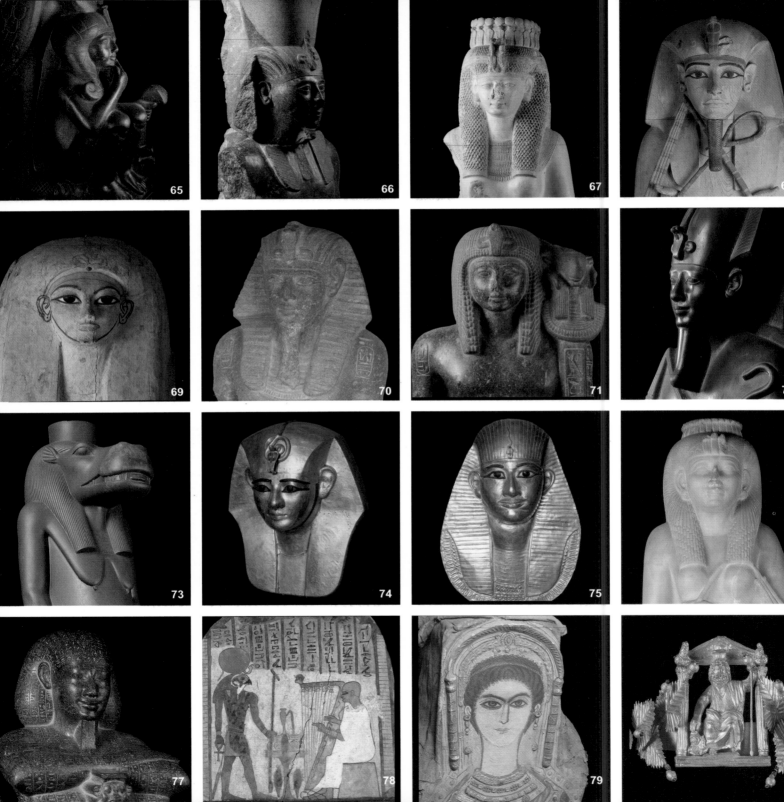

round pupils, five-toed forefeet and four-toed hind feet. But the tail hanging down the side of the shrine is long and straight; the club-shaped tip is more like a fox's brush than the curved tail of a dog, which is normally carried high up rather than low down like that of a jackal, wolf or fox. Carter claimed seeing a jackal-like dog in 1926 and in 1928, but both of them did not have the characteristic tail. This led him to believe that Anubis could be a jackal crossed with one of the dog species. Anubis was the most important of the three canine gods known in ancient Egypt. The other two were Wepwawet and Khentyamentiu. Anubis was the protector of the necropolis, who took part in the divine judgment. Anubis's association in the cemetery was probably due to the observation of the animals scavenging among the tombs. During the embalming and 'the opening of the mouth' rituals, the priests wore Anubis masks. From the New Kingdom on he was represented as a jackal-headed man and rarely appeared in a totally human form. The 'Pyramid Texts' of the Old Kingdom portray him as the Judge of the Dead. In many Old Kingdom mastaba tombs, the prAyr for survival after death was addressed to Anubis, as the god who led the deceased to the afterlife. Later when complemented with Osiris during the Middle Kingdom, he was credited with helping Isis and embalming Osiris, while still retaining his role as the Judge of the Dead. He is represented in Chapter 125 of the 'Book of the Dead' weighing the heart of the deceased against the *maat*. Originally Anubis was the local god of the 17th Upper Egyptian nome, named Cynopolis (city of the dogs) by the Greeks, eventually he was worshiped throughout the whole of the land. His four most important titles reflect his role: "He who is set upon his mountain" (to guard the necropolis); "Lord of the Necropolis"; "Chief of the Divine Pavilion" (where mummification took place); and "He who belongs to the mummy wrappings".

50. Accessories of the ceremonial chariot, Upper floor gallery 13.
51. Head of a Leopard, Upper floor gallery 9.
52. Figure of Weret Hekau, Upper floor room 3.
53. Detail of the Lion unguent container, Upper floor gallery 20.
54. Cow's head from the ritual couch of Mehet-Weret, Upper floor gallery 9.
55. Lion's head from the ritual couch of Mehtet, Upper floor gallery 9.
56. Hippo's head from the ritual couch of Ammut, Upper floor gallery 9.
57 & 58. Detail of the painted chest, Upper floor gallery 20.
59. Detail of the Throne, Upper floor gallery 35.

Carter found a wooden throne beneath the large funerary bed in the antechamber of the tomb. This is the only throne remaining from ancient Egypt. This piece of furniture is a fine example of the great skill of the craftsmen of the New Kingdom. It is made of wood covered with sheets of gold and inlaid with silver, semi-precious stones and coloured glass. The top of the front legs of the throne are in the form of a lion's head and the four legs are shaped like lion's paws. The arms are formed of crowned and winged serpents supporting the Pharaoh's cartouches with their wings as a sign of protection. On the back of the chair there is a depiction of the Pharaoh sitting in a relaxed manner on a chair. He wears a Composite Crown, a broad collar, long pleated kilt and the queen wears a long silver robe and a *uraeus* diadem surmounted by the sun disk, two feathers and two horns. She stands facing him tenderly touching his shoulders with her right hand. In her left hand she is holding a cup containing unguent. The Amarna style is evidenced by the portrayal of the Aten's rays to give them life. The name 'Tutankhamun' being written as 'Tutankhaten', while that of his wife is given as 'Ankhsenpaaten'. There are six *uraei* with crowns and solar disks, carved in wood and inlaid, situated between the vertical bars, which support the back.

60. Detail of the ornamented chest, Upper floor gallery 25.
61. Coffin of Tutankhamun's internal organs, Upper floor room 3.
62. Internal coffin of Tutankhamun, Upper floor room 3.

The mummy of Tutankhamun was laid inside the so-called innermost coffin, which was itself placed inside two further gilded wood coffins. These three coffins were then placed inside a stone sarcophagus. The king's mummy, the outermost coffin and the sarcophagus are still inside his tomb in the Valley of the Kings, while the middle and innermost coffins are in the Egyptian Museum in Cairo.

This middle coffin is made of gilded wood inlaid with glass and gems, and decorated with the images of the goddesses Isis and Nephthys stretching their wings around it in a protective fashion. The king is shown in the Osiris-form with his hands folded across the chest. On his head he wears the *nemes* headdress, on the forehead the typical *uraeus* and a vulture; on the chin he wears the false beard.

63. External coffin of Tutankhamun, Upper floor room 3.

Similar to the middle coffin, the innermost coffin has the Osiris-form with the arms crossed on the chest; the king holds in his hands the sacred insignia the *heka* sceptre and the *nekhaka* flail, symbols of righteousness and authority. Also similar to the middle coffin, the king wears the *nemes* headdress with the vulture and *uraeus* on the forehead, and a false beard on the chin. The inlaid eyes are missing. This coffin is made of solid gold and weighs 110 kilos. It is inlaid with glass and precious stones.

64. Canopic shrine, Upper floor room 9.
65. Detail of the statue of Ramses II as a child and god Horun.
19th Dynasty, reign of Ramses II 1304 - 1237. Ground floor, gallery 10.
66. Statue of Ramses II, Ground floor, gallery 10.
67. Bust of Queen Merit-Amun, Ground floor, gallery 15.
68. Coffin of Ramses II, Upper floor gallery 49.
69. Coffin of Sety I.
19th Dynasty, reign of Sety I 1317 - 1304 BC. Upper floor gallery 49.
70. Bust of Merenptah.
19th Dynasty, reign of Merenptah 1304 - 1237. Ground floor, gallery 13.
71. Statue of Ramses III as a standard bearer of Amun.
20th Dynasty, reign of Ramses III 1198 - 1166 BC. Ground floor gallery 15.
72. Statue of Osiris.
End of 26th Dynasty, *c.* 530 BC. Ground floor room 24.
73. Statue of goddess Taweret.
26th Dynasty, reign of Psametic I, 664 - 610 BC. Ground floor room 24.
74. Funerary mask of Amenemope.
21st Dynasty, reign of Amenemope 995 - 985 BC. Upper floor room 2.
75. Funerary mask of Psusennes I.
21st Dynasty, reign of Psusennes I 1043 - 994 BC. Upper floor room 2.
76. Statue of Amenirdis.
25th Dynasty, reign of Shabaka, 712 - 698 BC. Ground floor gallery 30.
77. Magical statue of Djed Hor.
Ptolemaic Dynasty, 305 - 31 BC. Upper floor gallery 13.
78. Harpist stela.
25th Dynasty, *c.* 850 BC. Upper floor room 22.
79. Mummy cover of a young lady.
Roman Period, 325 - 350 AD. Upper floor gallery 47.
80. Diadem with Serapis.
Roman Period, reign of Hadrian 117 - 138 AD. Upper floor room 4.

The Step Pyramid of Sakkara

Djoser was the first king of the Old Kingdom. He was one of the most famous of the early pharaohs, his name being revered and his spirit worshipped throughout Egyptian history. His great reputation of learning was perhaps due to the fact that his minister was the famous Imhotep, the philosopher, physician, architect and statesman, who was afterwards regarded as divine, and was ultimately identified with the Greek god of medicine, Asclepias. The king and his minister worked together; and the greatest of their achievements was the building of the Pharaoh's mighty tomb and mortuary temple at Sakkara.

The predecessors of Djoser were all buried in rectangular tombs known as *mastabas* built of sun dried bricks. They were all buried in Abydos and had built a cenotaph at Sakkara. However, Djoser was the first king to be buried in Sakkara and built the cenotaph at Abydos. The Step Pyramid is the oldest known pyramid in Egypt, it was constructed in the following manner. Upon the desert plateau the sand was cleared away and the flat surface of the underlying limestone was exposed over a wide area; and a large pit was then quarried in the rock nearly 24 m deep, with a rock-hewn stairway leading down into it. The bottom of the pit was lined with granite quarried at the First Cataract, nearly a 800 km to the south. These chambers and stairway and passage leading to them were then embedded in masonry up to the surface, and above them a great masonry was built, about 12 m high with side length of approximately 120 m. The blocks of limestone were quarried from the other side of the Nile. Upon this rectangular structure a second and a rather smaller rectangle was then built, and on this a third, fourth, fifth and sixth rectangle was constructed, each somewhat smaller than the one below, so that in the end the building assumed the appearance of a "Step Pyramid" in six steps, with total height approximately 60 m.

The Step Pyramid is regarded as the first large stone building raised on earth. It could be claimed without exaggeration that the Step Pyramid is a milestone in the evolution of stone building in Egypt and the whole world. A graffiti from the 19th Dynasty, in Sakkara, describe Djoser as "opener of stone" which means founder of stone architecture.

The first modern traveller to Djoser's Step Pyramid was the Prussian Consul-General von Minutoli, in 1821. He entered inside the pyramid and discovered the room with the blue fiancé. Inside the pyramid he found remains of a mummy with the inscription of Djoser. He sent these to Europe and the vessel was wrecked in a storm. Many years later fragments of the mummy were collected from the same place and were scientifically analysed. The result was that the method of wrapping and preservation was that of the Third Dynasty. Thus the lost mummy in the sea was likely to be that of Djoser.

Left and top right : when complete the Step Pyramid was a massive building consisting of 6 unequal steps with a total height of 62 m. Its base measures 123 X 107 metres.

Right : collonade at the entrance of Djoser's funerary complex. It contains 14 columns supported by pillars. The walls have small windows to allow in air and light. These columns were rebuilt by the French architect Philippe Lauer.

Left : **mastaba tomb of Niankhnum and Khnumhotep, 5th Dynasty *c.* 2400 BC, Sakkara.**
This scene shows the daily life of the Old Kingdom. It shows a fishing scene in two registers. The upper one shows fishermen pulling a net full of fish and some of them are dark-skinned Nubians. Some fishermen carry ropes around their necks and shoulders. They all pull the net together. On the right, another fisherman sits on a small papyrus boat and fishes with a hook. On the lower register a group of men are salting fish.

Top right : **mastaba tomb of Niankhnum and Khnumhotep, 5th Dynasty *c.* 2400 BC, Sakkara.**
A scene shows part of the daily life in the country side. One of the farmers is milking a cow with her little calf next to her. The rear legs are roped together to prevent her from kicking him. The text above is narrating the scene. We read also the name 'milk' which is *'jrt'* written with the determinative of the vase that always contained it. The farmer is seated naked, which was not an unusual thing. The cow is represented with horns from the face while her eyes from the profile, which is the canon of the Egyptian art. The target of the scene was to be a milk supply in afterlife, as it was thought that all these registers will come to be true by reciting magical forms narrated by the tomb visitors known as "calling of the living".

Right : **mastaba tomb of Kagemni, 6th Dynasty *c.* 2300 BC, Sakkara.**
The relief shows a farmer pulling a calf across a swamp, thus persuading its mother, and hence the whole herd to follow.

Left : **mastaba tomb of Kagemni, 6th Dynasty** *c.* **2300 BC, Sakkara.**
The scene here is an unusual representation of a bird-cage. We can recognize the frame of this cage made of many types of plants and branches of wood driven into the ground. A net is spread over that simple structure. Inside, a basin of water provided the birds with an area for exercise and water to drink. When the meal time came the farmer entered with a big bag full of cereal seeds on his shoulder, emptied it into a pile in front of the door in the eastern corner . Since the Old Kingdom, people privately kept different kinds of birds in cages such as geese, the mute swan *(Cygnus* sp.*)*, ducks, pigeons; chickens were known only from the Persian period starting around 525 BC.
The walls and the ceiling of the bird-cage itself are composed of a net of ropes spread between two wooden poles. A low door is placed on the right to allow the birds to go in and out easily. The centre is dominated by the pool of water where the birds can eat soaked food. The ancient Egyptians were very skilled in both animal and bird husbandry as are the farmers of Egypt today.
The Egyptians feared that the deceased might face famine in the netherworld after his resurrection and so that idea appears in funerary ritual beliefs. The huge supplies of food, the farming, fishing and breeding scenes aimed to provide for the dead in the afterlife by reciting magical formulas designated as "the calling of the living" which say: "You who live on the earth and serve people like me, may you repeat thousands of loaves of bread, of jars of beer, of bovines, and birds to our lovely friend (tomb owner), may you be in the company of gods".
From the artistic point of view, this scene illustrates the stylistic cannon of Egyptian art which ignores three-dimensional perspective. The bird-cage is represented with the horizontal and vertical dimensions but without depth. This type of representation aims at being a conventional form to imitate reality.

Top right : **mastaba tomb of Mereruka, 6th Dynasty** *c.* **2300 BC, Sakkara.**
A relief showing a crocodile hunt on a papyrus reed boat in the Delta marshes. On the background we see a screen of papyrus. The quick movement of the crocodile is depicted by a double drawing of its feet. The ancient Egyptians regarded the crocodile as a representation of the god Set, symbolising the evil and wickedness in the world. They considered killing the crocodile as a symbolic subduing of evil. Hence, the tomb owner would not be harmed as he entered the afterlife.

Right : **mastaba tomb of Mereruka, 6th Dynasty** *c.* **2300 BC, Sakkara.**
A relief shows dancing which was one of the ways to spend leisure time. It shows acrobatic movement, where dancers wear caps with a long tail ending with a round ball to stabilise their movement. Some types of dance had a funeral meaning like *maow* which was originally from Africa. It was performed before the burial to clear the tomb from bad spirits.

Mastaba tomb of Ptah-Hotep, end of 5th Dynasty *c.* 2380 BC, Sakkara.

Left : an excellent high relief still retaining its original colours. The two men in the foreground are carrying offerings of fowls and a gazelle on their shoulders. The man at the rear leads a calf tied to a rope and carries a slaughtered oryx and gazelle.

Above : excellent relief of Ptah-Hotep in a priestly costume and wearing a heavy wig typical of the Old Kingdom and is smelling a perfume. The feature of his face follows the Memphite school of art which is famous for its idealism. Strangely four of his fingers are shown same in size.

Top right : an excellent high relief of a hunting scene. A lion attacks a cow, which urinates in fear. The top register depicts a scene of gazelles, including a suckling fawn. The bushes in the background still retain their original green colour. The lower register depicts salted fish.

Right : the relief shows typical boat building showing workmen sewing the boat. The text above the scene records a conversation between workers saying "hey make room, your hand is under us". Small rafts were made of papyrus, while bigger boats were made of wood.

The Pyramids of Dahshur and Meidum

Snefru, founder of the Fourth Dynasty, came to the throne by marrying Queen Hetepheres, daughter of Pharaoh Huni. Snefru's mother was a member of Huni's harem. By marrying Huni's daughter, who was also his half-sister, Snefru confirmed by blood legitimacy his right to the throne. He was a legendary figure, and his reign seems to have been glorious. He is the father of Khufo builder of the Great Pyramid.

Snefru abandoned the royal necropolis at Meidum and chose the new site of Dahshur. Snefru is the only Pharaoh in Egypt who has four pyramids attributed to him It has been calculated that he used 3.7 million cubic metres of construction material. He completed the pyramid at Meidum, which had been started by his predecessor Pharaoh Huni. Then he abandoned the Meidum Pyramid. Some archaeologists speculate that his contribution to transfer the so far step pyramid into a true pyramid was unstable and the outer casing began to collapse. He then chose Dahshur, a new site closer to Memphis, to build his gigantic tomb. At Dahshur he built the Bent Pyramid and the Northern or Red Pyramid. The choice of Meidum must have been an intentional attempt to breach with some religious cults. His family may have had some links with the Fayoum region. Nefermaat, who was Pharaoh Huni's architect and Snefru's vizier, is buried in Fayoum. Nefermaat's son Hemiunu was Cheops's architect and was responsible for building the Great Pyramid. Hemiunu's tomb, which contains a statue of him, is in Giza. Snefru also built a fourth pyramid at Seila in Fayoum; this pyramid has no burial chamber and its remains are only seven metres high. The pyramid has been known for more than a hundred years, but its owner was identified only in the 1980's.

Left : the Bent Pyramid was planned from the beginning as a true pyramid, with its sides measuring 188.6 metres and with an original height of 101 metres. Its casing stone is the best preserved of all the pyramids of Egypt. The angle of slope is 54° 31′13′′ up to a height of 49 metres, and then it becomes 43° 21′. The change of the sloping angle gives the pyramid the name 'Bent Pyramid'. Archaeologists explain the change of the sloping angle by speculating that it was too steep to continue, and the centre of weight of the core masonry stones would make the structure unstable. Another explanation is that the builders may have felt that the casing stone was unstable and would fall out. However, cracks were discovered in the passage leading to the upper burial chamber. The builders tried to repair the damage by filling it with plaster. This might have been a strong reason for the builders to reduce the pyramid's slope. This modification resulted in reducing the weight of the upper part of the pyramid, thereby reducing the loads on the chambers and passages that had started to crack.

Top right : the Northern Pyramid at Dahshur also built by Snefru is the first true pyramid, with its slopes rising at a gentle angle of 43° 36′ instead of 52°. This became the standard angle of later pyramid's face inclination.

Right : the Pyramid of Meidum was a transitional stage of development from the step pyramid to the full pyramid. The tower-shaped pyramid was originally built as a step pyramid and later modified into a true pyramid by additional casing. This turned out to be a difficult task, and it collapsed. Several theories have been put forward to explain the reason for the collapse, for example that the pyramid was never finished and the collapse occurred during construction. This theory is based on the fact that the stelae at the temple near the pyramid was not finished and that the rough burial chamber was also left unfinished. The pyramid is surrounded by debris of its collapsed outer casing. The original entrance lies on the northern face, below the hole cut into the superstructure by ancient thieves. The pyramid was built by Huni, the last Pharaoh of the Third Dynasty, and completed by Snefru, the first Pharaoh of the Fourth Dynasty. Little of Huni's achievements are known. His name is in the canon of Turin but not on the Abydos list. No inscription of him survived

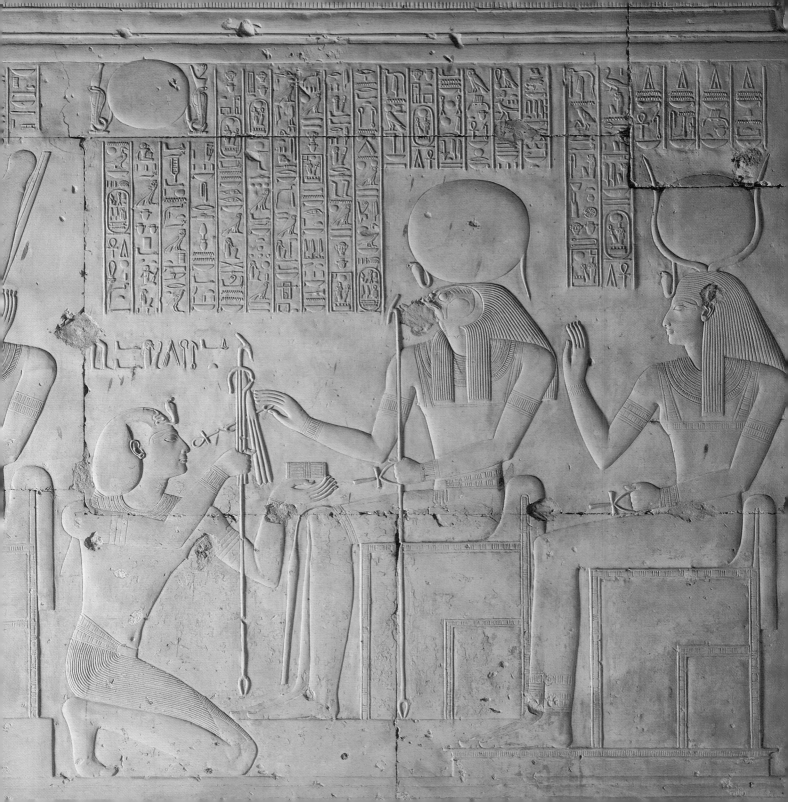

Temple of Sety I at Abydos

Abju of the ancient Egyptians was named Abydos by the Greeks. It is in the eighth nome of Upper Egypt. Since of dawn of history down to Byzantine Period Abydos was the holy city of Egypt. It is divided in three sections, the northern part contains the region of Kom el-Sultan, the temple of Osiris Khentymentiu, Umm el-Gaab, Shunet el-Zebib and the remains of funerary enclosures and cemeteries. The middle section has the temple of Sety I and temple of Ramses II. The southern part has ruins from the Middle Kingdom, the mortuary temple of Senusert III and the funerary complex of Ahmose I which consists of a pyramid and a mortuary temple. This pyramid is regarded the last pyramid built in Egypt.

The temple of Sety I lies south of Kom el-Sultan and was called "the house of the millions of years of the King *Mn-maat-Ra* who is rejoiced in Abydos". The construction of this temple marks the king's association with Osiris and in the same time is dedicated to the mortuary cult of the deceased king. The temple is famous for its L-shape form, as well as the gorgeous high reliefs of carving. Sety I was famous for the quality of his reliefs. We can see this from his reliefs at Karnak and his tomb at the Valley of the Kings. To-day this temple is regarded the most beautiful temple remaining from ancient Egypt. The temple is also famous for the King's List which lists 76 kings starting with Menes till Sety himself. Hatshepsut, Akhenaten,

Left : this is scene from the chapel of Ra Horakhty. The whole chapel has lost its colours. This scene is from the lower part of the southern wall. It shows Sety I giving sceptres and a bracelet to god Ra-Horakhty who in return hands him the *ankh* sign which is the key of life. The text explains the scene reading *"giving to Ra Horakhty mnfrt n rdwy"* meaning bracelet of legs or anklets. The facial features of the king show a quite smooth reflection and a deep emotions towards the god. Sety is shown here kneeling on the ground before Horus who is seated on the throne placed over a plinth destined for gods and kings.

Top right : the sanctuary of Ra-Horakhty. The seated god Atum is the evening form of Ra. The former is surmounted by the sun disk thus representing the midday form of Ra. The beetle *khepri* carved inside the disk, represents the early morning form of Ra. The verb *khepri* means self-birth or renewal. The ancient Egyptians observed that the scarab beetle emerged from balls of dung; that is why they associated it with the process of creation.

Right : the sanctuary from the Osiris complex on the northern wall. The king is represented here offering two banquets of blue lotus and papyrus reeds to Horus. The offering of lotus has a ritual significance as the lotus flower closes at dusk and reopens with sun rise, symbolising the cycle of the sun and the creation of the Universe according to Hermopolitan myth of creation. The text reads *"djd-mdw jn Hr, ntr nfr nb tawy, Mn maat-Ra, nb khaw, mry-n-Pth, Sty, d(w) ankh mj Ra".* which is a recitation to be said by Horus, the perfect god, the lord of two lands, *Mn maat-Ra* "may the justice of Ra sustain", the lord of crowns, the beloved of Ptah, Sety, may he be granted all life like Ra". It is interesting to note that Sety wrote his name in his cartouche using *tjt* sign of Isis instead of carving the god Seth as it is clear that the inscriptions tried to avoid it.

The king is represented wearing the necklace *wskh* to protect him in the afterlife and Horus is shown with the Double Crown of Upper and Lower Egypt. The scene is unusual because the king himself represents Horus ruling the earth.

Smnkh-Ka-Ra, Tutankhamun, Ay, Horemheb were omitted. Hatshepsut was cancelled because she had no legitimacy to the throne while the kings of the Amarna period were regarded as dammed.

Left : Sety kneeling before Ra-Horakhty with *uraeus* on the forehead and wearing *wskh* necklace as a sign of protection. The hieroglyphic verb *wskh* means to enlarge, hence the enlargement of offering and protection in afterlife. The king also wears bracelets and armlets and a short kilt. Ra-Horakhty is represented seated on his throne directing his right hand towards the king with the *was* sceptre of authority, the *djed* insignia of stability and finally the *ankh* key of life. In his left hand he is holding the *was* sceptre and *ankh* key of life. The throne is placed on a plinth made especially for gods. The king is presenting *maankht* offering, which is the lock of the chain.

The title of the scene is written horizontal above the king :"*rdt shpst maankht jn njswt*" meaning the giving the lock of the chain by the king to Ra-Horakhty.

Top right : this relief is from the chapel of Sety on its southern wall. This chapel make us believe that Sety considered himself sacred. In fact it had another purpose, because it represents the coronation of the king and his celebration of *Heb-Sed,* unlike the other chapels that show the daily rites of the temple. This chapel can be regarded as a mortuary chapel and also as a commemoration of the king.

In the scene we see the priest *jwn -mwt.f* burning incense before the king who has been carried by falcon-headed souls known as the 'souls of Buto' not visible in the picture. The priest here wears the usual panther garment and his hair has a side-lock. The 'souls of Buto' represent the sacred ancestors of Lower Egypt in Prehistoric times. Other opinions say that they could represent the spirits and powerful deities who helped the deceased king as well as in his lifetime. These souls were usually depicted with other souls called the 'souls of Nekhen', which was an important city in Archaic Egypt. Those souls were depicted with jackal heads.

Right : Sety burning incense in front of the god Horus in the sanctuary of Sety. He is holding in his left hand a jar filled with water, which he is pouring into a pot in front of Horus. The pot is decorated with a pair of blue lotus flowers. Horus holds in his right hand the *was* sign of prosperity and authority, and the *ankh* sign of life.

Temple of Hathor at Dendera

Hathor had many centre cults in Egypt, such as Serabit el-Khadim in Sinai, and a chapel in Abu-Simbel. However, the most famous centre was her temple at Dendera. The name Dendera was derived from *ta ntrt* meaning the goddess. In the Ptolemaic Period the name developed into Dendaris and in modern times to Dendera. The temple was occupied by the early Christians who turned the birth house into a church. A sacred marriage existed between goddess Hathor of Dendera and Horus of Edfu. In the annual festival the priests carried the sacred barge containing the statue of the goddess and sailed upstream to Edfu where she was united with Horus. This temple is famous for the Zodiac, now in the Louvre. The Astronomical ceiling depicting the solar cycle is shown in the Hypostyle Hall and Pure Chapel.

Left : the first Hypostyle Hall. The founding text of the hall on a frieze at the entrance mentions that Ptolemy XII had constructed the Hypostyle Hall but later some Roman Emperors had their own contribution. The most significant was Emperor Tiberius. The text inside the temple call this hall *'wskt-khnt'* meaning the front hall. It was not considered as a real part of the temple, because the public were allowed there in the festivals. The real sacred part of the temple begins with the second Hypostyle Hall. This hall has 24 columns arranged in six rows. They have Hathoric capitals in the form of sistrum. It is interesting to know that Hathor temple was called the house of sistrum. The dimensions of the hall is 42 X 26 metres. This hall is semi-closed by inter-columnar wall that allows light an air through. However, light and air was not allowed in the shrine that had the statue of the god. The Hypostyle Hall had the function of the sanctuary of the sacred barge. It was the meeting place for the gods of the temple as well as foreign gods. The faces of Hathor on the capitals has been vandalised by the early Christians as they were aware that she could harm them. Hathor was the goddess of motherhood, happiness, music, sex, fertility and alcohol. Till to-day women with fertility problems make offerings to Hathor.

Top right : the first appearance for the Hathoric capitals goes back to the Middle Kingdom. Later in the New Kingdom it was developed in two types of sistrum capitals. This one had a form of a sistrum but it was broken. The sistrum is a musical instruments that was much related to Hathor therefore Hathor was regarded goddess of music. The music had plAyd an important role in the ritual cult of the temple as playing with sistrum aimed to pacify the anger of Hathor. For example, in the prAyrs recited to the goddess we read : 'may your merciful face be towards me'. The sistrum was called *sshseshset,* derived from onomatopoeic name. The female priestess were musicians of the temple who were in charge of the accomplishment of the rites. The king himself had to play the sistrum to pacify the anger of the goddess.

Right : relief of Cleopatra her son Cæsarion and Ptolemy XIV before the goddess Hathor (not shown). This is the only known relief of Cleopatra and Cæsarion in an Egyptian temple. Ptolemy is wearing the *pschent* crown, which consists of the *hdjt* White Crown and the *dshrt* Red Crown. His head is also surmounted by a horned crown. Cleopatra holding a sistrum in the shape of Hathor and Amun, is offering incense. The purpose of this relief on the outer wall of the temple was political propaganda for Cleopatra's son to become the future king. It was a tradition in Greco-Roman temples to depict the king and queen as the same size, while in ancient Egyptian temples the queen was usually not shown on the outer walls of the temples, and if she was shown she was usually much smaller in size.

Luxor Temple

Luxor temple was founded in the Middle Kingdom, and was known as *ipet-rsyt* meaning the "secret sanctuary of the south" and was also known as the "great throne of Amun". The golden times of this temple was in the New Kingdom where the *opet* festival took place and also the celebration of the divinity of the king took place. Nectanebo I, 30th Dynasty, built an avenue of sphinxes with a length of about 3 km that connected Luxor and Karnak. Alexander the Great built a sanctuary for the barque of Amun. In the Roman period the site was turned into a garrison. Later in the Christian era the sanctuary of Alexander the Great was transformed into a basilica. In the 14th century a mosque dedicated to Abu el-Hagag was built on top of the open court of Ramses II.

This temple, like all temples in the east bank, is a cult temple. Temples on the west bank are funerary temples. In ancient times it was prohibited for commoners to enter inside the temples. Only in festivals they were allowed in the open courts.

Left : pylon of Ramses II, which is now the actual facade and entrance of the temple. The contribution of Ramses II in the temple is the 'First open court', the pylon, two colossal statues and an obelisk. Originally they were two obelisks, the second one was given in the beginning of the 19th century by Mohammed Aly, the viceroy of Egypt as a gift to France. The battle of Qadesh is carved on the pylon. However, it is now weathered away and is hardly recognisable. The pylon has four flag poles. The two colossal statues represent the *ka* of Ramses II. These massive monoliths reveal the divinity of Ramses II during his life time. The *ka* of the king inhabits the statue which always had names linked to Ra. For example "Ramses the beloved of Atum" or "Ramses the living image of Ramses beloved of Amun". Originally they were six statues, four seated and two standing, only three survived. The obelisk is placed on a pedestal which also has four baboons, who are supposed to yell at the rising sun. Ramses called the obelisk "Ramses beloved of Amun (the sun rising)".

Top right : seated statue of Ramses II in front of the colonnade of Amenhotep III. The king is seated with both hands on his thighs. The facial feature seem to reflect divinity of the sovereign, a slight smile appears on his lips. He wears the *pschent* or the Double Crown of Upper and Lower Egypt. On his right shoulder we read a cartouche of his name *Wsr-maat-Ra step-n-Ra* meaning the "the justice of Ra is powerful, chosen of Ra". On his left shoulder we read *Ra-mss* meaning the "born of Ra".

Right : Amenhotep III. had his own contribution to the temple, constructing the "Great Colonnade", the "Second open Court", the "Offering Hall", the sanctuary of the "Sacred barque" and the "holy of the holiest complex". These buildings were carried out by his architect Amenhotep son of Habu. The colonnade consists of 14 columns arranged in two rows. Their capital is an open papyrus form. This colonnade was started by Amenhotep III and completed by Tutankhamun, Ay and Horemheb.

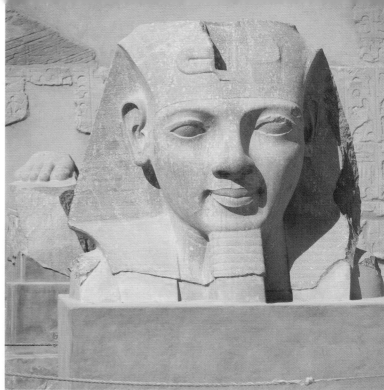

Left : Luxor temple.

Above : Pylon of Ramses II, built of sandstone 29 m high and 10 m thickness. The inscription reads that it was completed in the third year, the fourth month the third day of the *akhet* season. The battle of Qadesh is carved on the pylon.

Top right : colossal head of Ramses II in front of his pylon. It shows perfect facial features with a slight smile on his face with thick eye brows and a fleshy mouth. He wears the royal *nemes* head-dress. This head probably belonged to a colossal statue that stood in front of the pylon. The statue was fulfilling the function of the *ka* cult. The art in the 19th Dynasty is characterised with massive statues and taking care of many details.

Right : this sanctuary is in the middle of the western hall of offering. It was built by Amenhotep III to be a sanctuary for *wsrhat* the sacred barge. It is surrounded by a number of chambers and stores to keep the stock of the offerings and objects used during the daily service rituals of the temple. The items stored included vases, oil, incense, cloth and priest's garments. Amenhotep III is depicted on the walls of this sanctuary with the company of various gods specially on the eastern wall. This chapel once contained four columns which were removed by Alexander the Great in 332 BC in order to construct his own sanctuary for the barge of Amun. He is depicted on the inner and outer walls in the company of the Thebian Triad. We would like to add that Alexander the Great respected the architectural order of the temple as he built his chapel on the main axis. To-day this chapel is known as the chapel of Alexander the Great.

Karnak, the Great temples of Amun

The earliest remaining building in the site dates to the First intermediate Period at the reign of Antef II 2118-2069 BC. Building activities continued in the Middle Kingdom in the 11th and 12th Dynasty. The kings of the 11th Dynasty were natives of Thebes, and the city grew in importance under their rule and became the most important city in the country. However, the golden age of Thebes and Karnak was in the 18th and 19th Dynasty of the New Kingdom. In this period Egypt was the greatest imperial power of the world and she ruled the East. Egypt reached an unprecedented wealth and many tributes were pAyd by the subjects. In the Late Period Thebes had suffered a lot under the oppression from the foreign invaders. In the 25th Dynasty the Assyrian troops carried on a lot of destruction. In the year 666 BC. they violated the temples, broke the statues, vandalised the inscriptions and stole liturgical objects. The second invasion was carried out by the Persians in 525 BC. They persecuted the Egyptian Pantheon specially Cambyses who killed many priests of Karnak and plotted to kill the priests

Previous page : A panoramic view of the First Pylon built by Nectanebo I of the 30th Dynasty with the Avenue of the Sphinxes in the foreground. Each of the sphinxes has a ram's head on a lion's body. The ram as a symbol of fertility was the sacred animal of the god Amun. A small figure of the pharaoh Ramses II is placed between the paws of the lion to protect him and for him to be reborn in the afterlife from the flesh of this powerful animal. The number of complete sphinxes remaining is 33 in the southern row and 19 in the northern. The First Pylon consists of two towers; each has two sloping sides on which were affixed flags and royal signs during religious ceremonies. The Pylon symbolises *akht,* the horizon. The horizon was demonstrated as the sun disk between two mountains. Here the two mountains are represented by the two towers of the Pylon, and the sun disk by the god's statue inside the shrine.
Left : The Great Hypostyle Hall is composed of 134 columns arranged in 16 rows. The columns have papyrus-crown capitals. The height of each column is around15 metres not including the base. King Amenhotep III had 12 of these erected, while Kings Sety I and Ramses II added the other 122 columns. The hall is enclosed by a wall, which has small window openings to let in light and air. The Great Hypostyle Hall is one of the marvels of New King-

dom architecture. It never fails to inspire visitors as even we in modern times feel dwarfed in comparison to the achievements of the ancient Egyptians. Here one can grasp the concept of immortality in art through a civilisation.
Above : A scene from the open court of the temple of Ramses III. This court was intended to represent the king in the Osirian form. The king had to pass a transformation into the immortal deity Osiris. The massive construction of the temple and the statues tell us about the stability and wealth of the country under Ramses III. The caryatides and pillars represent the king in mummified form holding two sceptres. Each has a vertical hieroglyphic column declaring the royal titles. They were dedicated to worship the gods of the temple. On the east side they were dedicated to Thoth, Sobek, Ptah, Horakhty, Amun and Mut. Those on the west side were dedicated to Seth, Ra Horakhty, Khonsu, Mout and Montou. The total number of statues are 16 with 8 on each side. The inscription inside the temple reads "Ramses, the prince of Heliopolis, he blessed the sanctuary of the barge of Amun, named *akhet*, the mysterious, that was built in the sacred place on the divine soul". The text continues "The nobles rejoice when they saw the king establishing the temple, this perfect monument where he reigned in this sacred place and his heart was rejoiced with this masterpiece".

of the oracle in Siwa. On his way from Kharga Oasis to Siwa with an army of 50 000 men they faced a sand storm and were all killed. Till this day no trace of his army was ever found.

Karnak is arranged in two axis, one from west to east and the other from north to south. Both axis meet at the central part of the temple where four obelisks were placed. This complex of temples was dedicated to the Thebian Triad consisting of Amun, his wife Mut and their son Khonsu. The region dedicated to Amun is the greatest part of the temple and is now open to the public. The region dedicated to Mut is at the south, and the northern part is dedicated to Montu, who was the original god of Thebes before Amun. Montu is the god of war. The axis of west to east contains from the First to the Sixth Pylon where the sanctuaries of the sacred barge of Amun is to be found. The axis from north to south contains from Seventh to Tenth Pylon. This temple was known as *jpt- rswt* since the time of king Sesostis II, meaning the 'chosen site'. In the Ptolemaic Period it was named *pt- hr- sa-ta* meaning the sky over the land.

The current entrance is from the west - east axis. The First Pylon at the entrance was built by Nectanebo I. The Second Pylon was built by Horemheb and completed by Ramses I. The Third Pylon was built by Amenhotep III, and is now in total ruins. The Fourth Pylon dates to Tuthmosis I. The Fifth and Sixth Pylon goes back to Tuthmosis III. The north-south axis starts with the Seventh Pylon that was built by Tuthmosis III. The Eighth Pylon was built by Hatshepsut and Tuthmosis III. The Ninth and Tenth Pylon were built by Horemheb and Akhenaten. In golden age, 80000 priests served in the temples.

Left : the sacred lake dug by Amenhotep III. The lake was full of geese, because it was a sacred bird of Amun. The main purpose of the lake was ablution before entering the temple.

Top right : this statue of Ramses II is sculpted out of granite and is in perfect condition. Here the king is depicted with one of his daughters probably *Pnt-ant,* standing between his feet. The king wears the *pschent* crown which is composed of the Crowns of Lower and Upper Egypt; he is holding the *heka* sceptre symbol of authority and the *ms* sceptre symbol of rebirth. The statue is colossal in size, which was the tradition in art of the Ramesside period. This statue has been usurpated first by King Ramses VI from the 20th Dynasty who had his name carved on the base, later King Panijm from the 25th Dynasty added his name.

Right : a scene from the temple of Ptah showing Ptolemy IV who reigned from 222 - 205 BC with the queen standing behind him. The king is wearing the double crown and the inscription in front of him reads "Making adoration to Ptah four times". The text above the king says "May he (or she) be given life as Ra, the beloved of god". Ptah is shown standing in his shrine holding the sceptres of *was, ankh* and *djed*.

Valley of the Kings
Tomb of Tuthmosis III (1504 – 1450 BC) KV 34

The tomb of Tuthmosis III was discovered in 1898 by the French archaeologist Victor Loret. The entrance lies in a recess in the rocks approximately 20 metres above the valley floor. This ingenious site is concealed naturally and in addition rains and floods had piled up debris that further hid the tomb. Today the entrance is reached via a steel stairway, but at the time the tomb was built the stairs were built of mud brick. From the top of the stairs one has a beautiful panoramic view of the royal valley. The entrance points to the north and the burial chamber lies on an east-west axis. The burial chamber is not rectangular but oval in shape, 15 X 9 metres and has four side chambers; their purpose was for the funerary offerings. The well chamber is an innovation to the previous tombs.

Left : The cartouche shaped sarcophagus of Tuthmosis III, in the burial chamber. It is made of yellow quartz and painted in red to imitate granite. The cartouche-shape is derived from the *shen* sign which means eternity hence the intention to achieve that for the king. The picture shows the eastern side of the sarcophagus. The horizontal cartouche at the top reads : "text recited by Osiris, my son, the King of Lower and Upper Egypt, the lord of making rituals, *Mn-Khprw-Ra*, the heir, the governor of the west, Horus the born of Isis, her arms are around you, may you live forever son of the sun Tuthmosis, the true voice around Osiris" . We find five cartouches represented vertically. From left to right : "reading to be recited by Mehen, the pacified one concerning this matter, the beloved by the King Tuthmosis". Mehen is a coiled serpent protected by Ra; he, in turn offered protection to the deceased king through special spells to be recited. The second cartouche reads "The perfect god, lord of two lands, lord of making rituals, king of Lower and Upper Egypt *Mn-khprw-Ra* the true voice, the lord Osiris." The third cartouche is similar to the second except for the title of son of the sun Tuthmosis. The fourth cartouche says "The good lord, lord of two Lands, lord of making rituals, the king of Lower and Upper Egypt *Mn-khprw-Ra* the true voice before the lord Osiris". The fifth cartouche says "Reading to be recited by Sokker, I grant happiness to King Tuthmosis". The deities represented on the sarcophagus from left to right are gods Imesti, Anubis and Duamutef. Imesti is represented as a man and the columns next to him is a text he is supposed to read. Anubis and Duamutef are supposed to read the text to their left. Both of Imesti and Duamutef are two of the four sons of Horus, depicted on the sarcophagus, as they were in charge of introducing the deceased king to the sky. They also were named "the friends of the king".

Top right : this scene from the *Amduat* is on the left pillar of the burial chamber. It shows the deceased king in the solar barge with Isis and preceded by emblems. On the lower right corner we see the king as a child sucking from Isis depicted as a sycamore tree. The column behind the king says "*Mn-khprw-Ra sq.f mwt.f Ast"* meaning his mother Isis is suckling the king. The text, not visible in the picture, is written in cursive style with both red and black ink to imitate an open papyrus.

Right : iron stairs leading to the tomb which lies in a deep cliff situated above the valley floor. The idea of placing the tomb at the foot of the mountain is to accumulate debris and gravel from rain floods, to conceal the entrance.

Tomb of Tutankhamun

The world famous tomb of King Tutankhamun is the smallest of the kings' tombs; it was discovered in 1922 by the English archaeologist Howard Carter. It was found to be richer in treasures than any other tomb hitherto discovered, since it had never been looted by grave robbers, even in ancient times. Tutankhamun was nine years old when he came to the throne. At the beginning of his reign, when his name was still Tutankhaten, he lived at Tell el-Amarna where Akhenaten had established a new city for the worship of the Aten. But the young king, who was the second successor to Akhenaten, in obedience both to public opinion and to the priests of Amun, re-established the royal residence in Thebes, and at the same time changed his name to Tutankhamun.

Left : overall view of the burial chamber, with the sarcophagus and coffin. The walls which are coloured yellow have a decoration that is very similar to that in the tomb of Ay.
From left to right we see the king and his *ka* before Osiris. The *ka* is shown as a separate figure wearing the emblem of its identity on its head. It means: 'Horus the powerful bull'. This whole scene is placed in hieroglyphs inside the *ka* sign, which is two raised hands. He wears a false beard, which is a characteristic of the *ka*. The text above the king says: "*Nebkhepru-Ra*, granted life and stability forever, the Great God, Lord of Two Lands, Lord of Crowns". The text above the *ka* reads : "Replacing the royal *ka* from the front".
The next scene shows the king with goddess Nut wearing a white dress with a red belt. She is performing the *nini* ritual, a type of greeting and purifying rite. The water above her hands inviting him to the west is in a zigzag form like the letter N. The text above Nut says: "Mistress of the Sky, may she carry out the *nini* greeting for her newborn, may she have all health and life". The king is holding in his right hand two royal insignias, the *ankh*, and the papyri-form mace, symbols of life and light respectively. In his left hand he holds a *mks* staff.
The next scene shows King Ay garbed in a priest's robe and performing the ritual of 'the opening of the mouth' on Tutankhamun in the mummy-Osirian form. The tools used in the ritual are placed on a table between the two kings. This rite had a political significance as the new king had to perform it on the deceased king in order to legitimise his claim to the throne. We know that Ay usurped the throne following Tutankhamun's sudden death leaving no direct heirs.
Top right : the First Hour of the *Amduat* with 12 baboons and the early morning representation of the sun god Ra as a beetle. The First Hour of the *Amduat* starts when the gates of heaven open for the setting sun to sink beyond the horizon to the realm of the dead, the netherworld. In this moment light falls in the dark underworld, and reflects back to our world for a short period until total darkness prevails. The appearance of the sun in the netherworld is greeted with dancing and music by a group of 12 baboons. They speak a secret language that only the sun god Ra and the dead understand. Their number is 12 because it coincides with the number of night hours.

Right : a scene from the south wall of the burial chamber, where Tutankhamun is standing between Hathor and Anubis. Hathor is represented as a beautiful young woman wearing a long white dress and red belt around her waist with two long bands. She also wears the *wskh* necklace and bracelets and carries the *imentet* western emblem on her head. It consists of a standard topped by a falcon and a feather. The falcon that perches on top of the *imentet* sign refers to the sun setting in the west. The text above her says "Hathor mistress of the sky, the mistress of west." The king is represented wearing a short white kilt very decorative and a pair of white sandals. He is receiving the *ankh* key of life from Hathor. The text above the king says "The good lord *Nb khprw-Ra* may he grant life and stability for ever". The text to the right of Anubis says "Anubis the first of the Westerners the good god, the supervisor of mummification." and the text behind him reads "Isis mistress of the sky is performing *nini* ritual to the one she gave birth, may she grant him all health."

Tomb of Ramses I, KV16

Ramses I is the founder of the 19th Dynasty. His career was in the army, and he came to the throne as an old man, therefore his rule was brief less than two years. Hence his tomb is small and simple. It consists only of a burial chamber. Its artistic style and colours are very similar to the tomb of his predecessor Horemheb. One can think that both tombs were made by the same artists. The illustration in the tomb are only from the Book of Gates. The way of art performed in paintings was according to the orthodox way of art prior to Amarna. He wanted to wipe out all traces of Akhenaten's heresy.

Left and top right : the beginning of the Fourth Hour of the 'Book of Gates'; it starts with a gate guarded by a snake coloured yellow. Four men pull the sun barge along the river of *Duat*, with the sun god Ra standing inside a shrine on the barge, surrounded by the multi-coiled serpent 'Mehen', which means the 'encircle'. Two men also stand on the barge, one at the bow and the other at the rear. The former symbolises Sia or 'mind - perception', while the latter represents heka or 'magic'. The solar barge passes by a series of nine shrines with mummies inside *(top right)*. The horizontal form of the mummies is to show that they are in a deep sleep of death.

The multi-coiled snake in the middle register represents the passage of time. The red coloured sea in the lower register symbolises the sea of fire, which was referred to often in the Coffin Texts and formed part of the netherworld landscape. It is sometimes referred to as a *uraeus* sea or in the Sixth Hour as a "cavern of fire". This is not yet the place of punishment, for the blessed dead, it is the "Sea of Life", which quenches their thirst.

Right : a scene from the back wall showing Osiris standing inside a shrine in his mummy-form with his foot on the Apophios snake. In front of Osiris is his title: "Khentyamentiu, the First of the Westerners". Two protective gods are represented to the left and right of the shrine. On the left is Anubis represented as a ram-headed man and on the right is the *uraeus*. It was most unusual to represent Anubis with a ram's head. Apophios must be killed because he is an enemy threatening the night journey during the Fourth and Fifth Hours.

Tomb of Tausert and Setnakht, KV14

This tomb begun under Sety II in his second year of reign has an exciting history. He built the tomb for his 'Great Royal Wife' Tausert, a privilege or particular right not given to just any queen. Even Ramses II did not concede this privilege to his beloved Queen Nefertary.

When Siptah died Tausert declared herself queen, exactly as Hatshepsut had done 300 years earlier. The tomb was extended by Tausert, planning it to be a true royal tomb decorated with themes from the books of the netherworld. In addition she built a second burial chamber larger than the existing one. However, her reign was not accepted and in 1185 BC the elderly prince Setnakht appeared as a saviour. His exact relationship to the royal house is unknown, but he could have been one of the sons of Ramses II, who had died only 20 years earlier. In his short reign of two years, he re-established law and order, and was the founder of the powerful 20th Dynasty.

The tomb was later seized by Setnakht, but all he did was to have the drawings and cartouches of Tausert replaced with those of himself.

Left : the Sarcophaga's hall of Queen Tausert. The registers on the walls are from the 'Book of the Gates'. On the pillars protective deities are represented. On the top of each pillar a *kheker* motive is drawn, its origin stems from pre-history. On the first pillar from the left Geb is shown with a false bear. He is the earth god in the Theology of Heliopolis. On the second and third pillars Anubis is guarding the entrance. On one of them his titles are written and the other one is without any text. Horus son of Isis is depicted on the fourth pillar. All four gods are looking towards the entrance to welcome the deceased. On the lower register funerary equipment are drawn such as jewelry boxes, shrines, vases of oil and perfumes.

Top right : a scene from the sarcophagus hall on the southern wall. It has a complete version of the Book of Earth where we can see the resurrection of the sun-god at the end of the night. He is represented in a mummy-form and is also represented in the upper register lying horizontally and surrounded by the sun disk and stars. The main concept in the Book of Earth (*Aker*) is to highlight the triumphant rebirth of the sun. Piankoff has named this book "Creation of the Solar Disk" because the sun is raised from the depth of the night where the dammed dead are punished.

Right : the Tenth Hour from the 'Book of Gates'.

The theme of the Tenth Hour deals with the fight against Apophis, while the text describes the union between Ra and Osiris. The scene in the upper register has a strong symmetry with the double sphinxes at its centre. Both wear the White Crown of Upper Egypt. A double-headed 'being' stands on the backs holding the heads of both Horus and Seth. 'Horus in the barge' is pulled by the gods of Upper and Lower Egypt using imaginary ropes; each group wearing the respective crown. In the middle register, the task is the punishment of the cursed dead and Apophis. Magic is used to fulfil this duty. A single rope connects all the figures in the lower register. The rope pulls the sun barge through the netherworld. The first four gods on the left represent the ba spirits of the westerners, these are then followed by the three figures of Thoth, Horus and finally Ra. On the right-hand side (not shown in the picture), the rope is tied in the form of a double snake with two heads and one pair of legs. On the lower register a serpent rests on a pair of quick moving legs. All are connected to another symmetrical pair of snakes. In the centre sits Horus, king of the netherworld, who in the text is described as 'Khepri'. Here the dawn is beginning and the sun is on its way to be reborn.

Tomb of Ramses III, KV11

This tomb has a strange plan unlike his predecessors. The entrance is a central ramp surrounded by a stair-case. The first section of the tomb was done by Setnakht, but as work intersected with tomb of Amenmeses KV10, he abandoned the site. His son Ramses III started again work and made it his own burial. He moved the tomb's axis by 2 metres to avoid intersecting with KV10. This tomb is one of the longest in the Valley of the Kings measuring over 180 metres.

The decorations are in low relief and are in a good state of preservation. The Litany of Ra, parts of the *Amduat* and also parts of the Book of Gates decorate the first corridor. The decoration of the burial chamber is in a poor state because rain floods drowned the place. But it still has some traces from the Book of Gates and the Book of Earth.

Left : a scene shows part of the first pillared hall with central ramp leading to the lower corridor. The king is shown on the pillars making offerings to several deities.

Top right : the column on the facing right side of the pillars show the king wearing a kilt with decorative motives and a band across his shoulders. He is holding a pot of *rmj* perfume oil. The text behind him says "Protection, life may surround him forever". His two titles are listed in front of him "Ramses, the ruler of Heliopolis" and his coronation name "*wsr-maat-Ra mry -jmn*" meaning is the justice of Ra beloved by Amun. The column below says "I give *rmj* (kohl) to god".

Right : a blind harpist in one of the small side chambers. It was this drawing copied by the Englishman James Bruce in the 1760's, which became a popular scene in Britain.

Funerary music helped restore the deceased back to life. Here the harpist is holding a *bnt* harp. the deity of the harpist was called "*Khenty-N-Jrty*" meaning the Blind Horus, to confirm the fact that most harpists were blind.

Tomb of Ramses IV, KV2

This tomb is in a perfect state; the corridors and the antechambers contain the Litany of Ra, sections from the Book of the Dead and the Book of Caverns which appeared for the first time in the tombs. In the burial chamber the walls are covered by the Book of Heavens, sections from the *Amduat* and the Book of Gates. Goddess Nut is demonstrated in the astronomical ceiling. This tomb has hundreds of graffiti written in Greek, Coptic and Latin. The coptic graffiti reveal that an early Christian community lived in the tomb.

Left : entrance corridor leading to the burial chamber decorated with scenes from the 'Book of Caverns' and the 'Book of the Earth'.
Right : the burial chamber's flat ceiling has two scenes of the goddess Nut stretching her body across the vault of the heavens and swallowing the sun disk at dusk, then travelling through her body at night to be reborn again the following morning.

Mortuary Temples of Thebes

The mortuary temples are all built on the West Bank of the Nile. They are all named "house of million years", and they were dedicated to the royal *ka*. On the west bank many important festivals were celebrated, the most important is the "beautiful festival of the valley" which was related to goddess Hathor as she was the mistress of the west and she was the one who welcomed the deceased king into her realm. This festival took place in the second month of *shmw* summer season. The target of this festival was to reach the sanctuaries of Hathor in Deir el-Bahary. In antiquity a canal connected the mortuary temples to the Nile. Each of the temples had its proper name such as *djeser djeserw* for Deir el-Bahary meaning "holy of the holiest". The Rameseum was called "united with Thebes", and Medinet Habu was called "united with Eternity". Each temple had an enormous number of priests in charge of the daily service of the royal *ka* cult. Also each temple sustained its own economy by owning a fertile land that generated income.

The Temple of Queen Hatshepsut

This temple, dedicated to the cult of "the beautiful and gifted" Hatshepsut and her family, differs in plan, style of architecture and decoration from all other temples in Egypt. It is more graceful, pleasing and certainly less oppressive, freer in its style, than the monumental and massive buildings of the previous periods. It is worth noticing that it was a woman who finally broke through the established tradition of temple architecture.

The temple was dedicated to the god Amun but it contained also chapels for the god of the dead, Anubis, and for Hathor, the tutelary goddess of the Theban necropolis. There are few buildings remaining anywhere in which the struggle for power within a family can be so clearly traced as in this temple. Queen Hatshepsut (1498 - 1483 BC) had built it, but in every place on its walls and pillars where her lineaments or her name appeared, her features and her appellations have been chiselled out and effaced. It was her step-son Tuthmosis III who thus satisfied his hatred and wreaked his vengeance on his co-regent.

Left : panoramic view of the mortuary temple of Hatshepsut. We can notice the three terraces all carved in the mountain. It was her brilliant architect Senmut who designed and built this temple. Probably the design was inspired from an ancient building by Mentuhotep II from the 11th Dynasty some 500 years earlier. The chapel of Mentuhotep was discovered by Howard Carter. The temple had a wide causeway about 30 m across, it connected the barge shrine with the temple, especially during festivals. Exotic trees that Hatshepsut brought from Punt (Somalia) were planted in the First open court that preceded the first ramp.

Top right : high relief of soldiers at the Hathor shrine. The soldiers accompanied the expedition of Punt to protect its members. They are carrying the goods of Punt.

Right : scenes from Punt showing its landscape and huts of natives approachable only through a ladder, probably to protect them from wild beasts and also to be away from the ground that is constantly washed by rain showers. The whole village lies on the sea shore therefore the water drawing in the lower part of the scene.

Left : the colossi of Memnon were originally in front of the First Pylon of the mortuary temple of Amenhotep III. The temple was destroyed in an earthquake in the 27 BC, and its ruins were removed by the locals. The statues are about 23 m high. Judging from the size of the statues, the temple must have been enormous. The statues were named Memnon from the Greek tourists who thought that they personify the Ethiopian hero Memnon who was killed by Achillas in the Troy war. The statues represent instead the king seated on his throne, in the northern statue he is with his mother Mutmwaya and the southern statue represents the king with his wife Tye. The southern colossal was called "ruler of the ruler" and it had its own cult. The *sematawy* sign is carved on the side of the throne, it shows Hapi joining the plants of Upper and Lower Egypt together. The temple was designed and built by the architect Amenhotep son of Hapu, he also supervised the transportation of the colossal stones of the statues. The architect was defied in the Late Period. Thousands of Graffiti are inscribed in Greek and Latin by tourists of antiquity. After one of the statues had been damaged by the earthquake it is said that every morning shortly after sunrise it emitted certain sounds. Travellers called it a song. The portion of the colossus that has been damaged in the earthquake was restored under Septimius Severus by building it up with blocks of stone, and this caused the sounds to cease.

Top right : the pylon of Medinet Habu. The site lies at the southern edge of the west bank known as Kom el-Hitan. It was considered holy and a place of pilgrimage. It was known in the Egyptian texts as *djme* meaning "the sacred hill". The site had a mythical significance from the myth of Hermopolis. A chapel to the god Amun-Ra Kamutef was built by Tuthmosis III and Hatshepsut. The holiness of this site attracted Ramses III to construct his funerary temple named "Ramses III united to Eternity". The pylon was built by Ramses III and now it is the entrance to the temple. However, the original entrance was next to the chapel of Tuthmosis III. The pylon depicts Ramses III smiting enemies. On the southern tower the king is offering the captives to Amun-Ra who gives him back the sword *khepesh*. Goddess who personifies Thebes is holding a rope tied to the captives. Below the names of defeated towns are listed. On the northern tower is a similar scene showing also the king smiting the enemies, who were the sea people, the names mentioned were *Mashwash,* now the Amazerian, *Sheklesh* from Sicily, *Sheredana*, now Sardenia. An error was recorded on that tower in carving African names of fallen towns and meanwhile carving people with Asian features. The words of the inscription quote Ramses III "Say to the defeated chief of Mshwash, see how your name is destroyed forever and how your mouth is ceased of saying rebellion at the mention of Egypt by the might of my father lord of lords."

Right : part of a second court shows perfect reliefs of coloured paintings on the papyrus-shaped columns that support the architraves. Isis is touching Ramses III, and she is surmounted by her title "mistress of all gods". The text in front of her reads "I grant you millions of *heb-sed* and hundred thousand years." The king is wearing the Blue Crown *khprsh* of war and is offering milk to the deity.

Aswan and Abu Simbel

Aswan is Egypt's southernmost winter resort, attracting travellers from all over the word. The scenary at Aswan is fascinating. It is one of the bright, cheerful spots of Egypt, if not the brightest. Elephantine Island and the temple of Philae are among the places of special importance in this region. 220 km south, at Abu Simbel, there are the two rock temples built by Ramses II, one of the most magnificent memorials of ancient Egypt.

Left : Elephantine Island with the Aga Khan Mausoleum in the background.

Top right : temple of Isis located originally on Philae island. In 1970 the temple was moved from its original island to its present place on Agilika island. This island at First Cataract consists of red granite. It combines a complex of temples of Isis and Hathor as mistress of foreign lands. It has ruins dating to Nectanebo I of the 30th Dynasty. The summit of its activity was in the Greek-Roman Period. The Kiosk of Emperors Trajan and August is still in a good state. The island was a holy place of pilgrimage till the 6th century. The island was one of the most important centres that survived Christianity till the 6th century. Finally they were defeated by the Byzantine Emperor Justinian. The latest prayer recorded in the temple was in 473 AD, and also the last known hieroglyphic text to be inscribed in Egypt was on this island in 395 AD. The beautiful hypostyle hall was turned into a church with the inscriptions and pictures on the walls being plastered over with Nile mud, for the eyes of the faithful to be preserved from pollution. Then Nubians were forced to Christianity.

Right : facade of the temple of Nefertari at Abu Simbel, who was the most famous wife of Ramses II. The temple was dedicated to the Hathor cult and Nefertari. The facade consists of six colossal statues, three on each side of the entrance. Ramses II is flanking the entrance wearing the crown of Upper Egypt. Next to him are statues of Nefertari wearing the horns of Hathor as goddess of love. On the far sides Ramses is once wearing the White Crown of Upper Egypt and in the opposite side wearing the crown of Amun. The inscription on the facade reads "Son of the sun the good lord, the ruler of the two lands, the lord of crowns, the beloved one Ramses, the beloved of Amun *Wsr-mat-Ra-stp-n Ra* (coronation name)".

Nexr page : temple of Ramses II at Abu Simbel. The facade is composed of four colossal statues of Ramses II seated on the throne with daughters and wives sculpted much smaller in size at his feet. The ingenuity of this temple is that it is carved from a single piece of rock. A frieze of cobra and baboons surmount the facade. The colossal statues reflect the political influence of Egypt in Upper Nubia. Ramses's father Sety I carved a rock-cut temple at KanAys in the Eastern Desert. Abu Simbel was dedicated to the state gods Amun-Ra, Ra-Horakhty, Ptah and the king himself. Due to an earthquake the head and crown of one of the statues has fallen on the ground. Many graffiti are inscribed on the statues written by soldiers of the Libyan kings of the 21st Dynasty. In the centre of the facade Ramses II is carved offering the *maat* sign to Ra Herakhty in his niche. The battle of Qadesh is carved on the walls inside the temple. The peace treaty between Ramses and the Hitites was carved on a stela and placed in front of the temple but it had disappeared in antiquity.